ABLE-BODIED SEAMEN

MARINES

CIVILIANS

CAT-BUILT COLLIER

94 PEOPLE ABOARD (BUILT FOR 16)

COMMISSIONED BY THE BRITISH ROYAL NAVY
SOUTH PACIFIC TO OBSERVE THE TRANSIT OF
ELUSIVE TERRA AUSTRALIS INCOGNITA, THE
JOSEPH BANKS PAID 10,000 POUNDS FOR HIS
TO COLLECT NEW PLANT AND ANIMAL SPECIES.

To Sir Thomas Masterman Hardy
(1769 – 1839), baronet and British naval officer,
and to all his descendants, of whom I am one. – GB

This edition first published in 2018 by Gecko Press
PO Box 9335, Wellington 6141, New Zealand
info@geckopress.com geckopress.com

© Gavin Bishop 2018
© Gecko Press Ltd 2018

Gecko Press gratefully acknowledges the support of Creative NZ.

creativenz
ARTS COUNCIL OF NEW ZEALAND TOI AOTEAROA

Typeset in Pabst L and Quimbly
Illustrations created in watercolour and acrylic ink on paper

Design and typesetting Vida Kelly
Printed in China by Everbest Printing Co. Ltd,
an accredited ISO 14001 & FSC certified printer

ISBN 978-1-77657-204-5 hardback
ISBN 978-1-77657-217-5 limited edition of 100 copies

GAVIN BISHOP

Cook's Cook

The Cook who Cooked for Captain Cook

GECKO PRESS

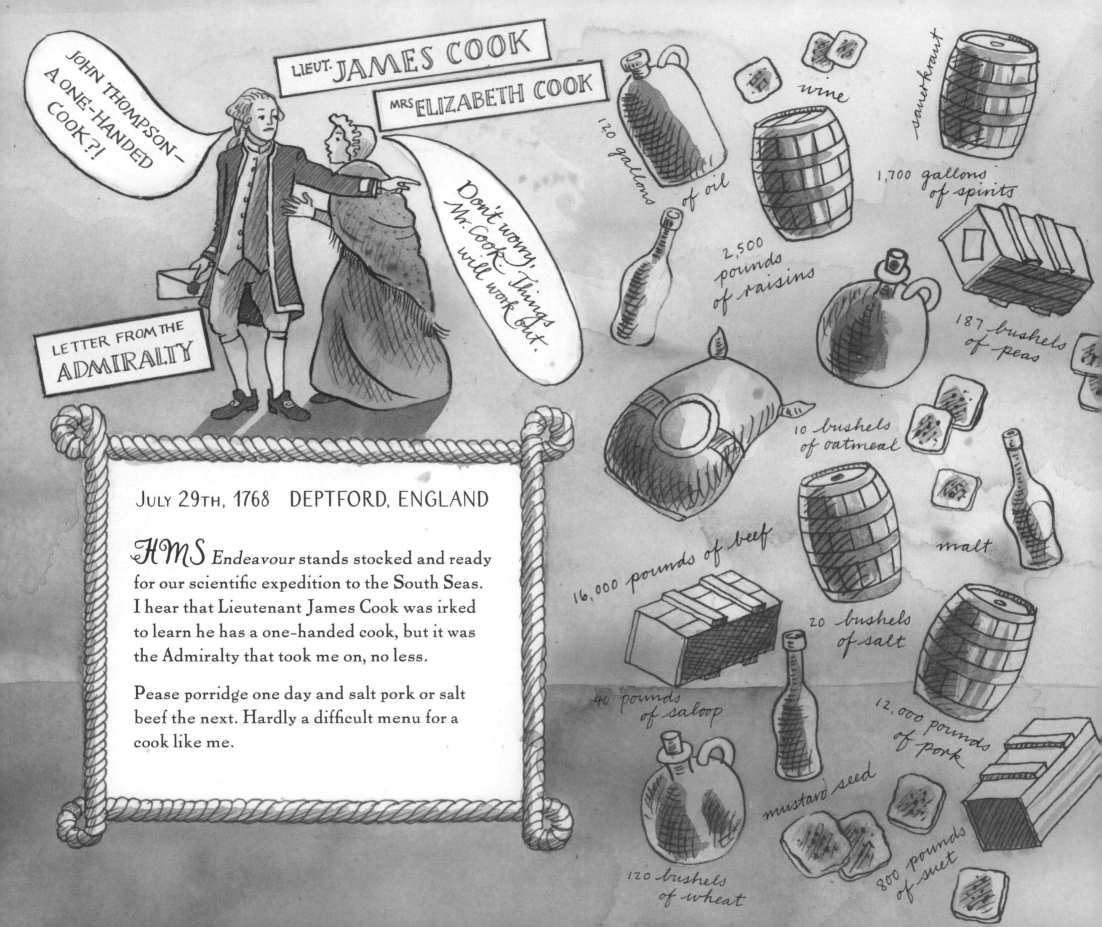

AUGUST 26TH, 1768   PLYMOUTH, ENGLAND

The *Endeavour* sailed out of Plymouth this afternoon.

My galley's on the mess deck. The men sling their hammocks here at night, but they have to be gone by eight in the morning so I can make breakfast.

After breakfast, one man from each table helps me out. I give him his table's ration of flour, suet and raisins to mix the puddings. Then he labels the pudding bags and drops them in the boiler alongside the meat—all in together. Come dinnertime, he serves up for his messmates. In the great cabin above, the lieutenants have their own cook who prepares their evening meals.

Dinner's at midday, followed by tobacco time— smoked or chewed. Then I put out the fires. In the evening, the grog comes out and the men eat leftovers.

Each man has brought a bowl, plate, spoon and mug on board. I give him a good square meal on his own square plate. If he's still hungry, I tell him to eat wind pudding!

The captain has a supply of fine china, glassware, silver cutlery and linen tablecloths, in case of visitors. The gentlemen have brought their own extras—special meats, wines and cheese. It's all right for some.

SEARED SHARK STEAKS

Cut wide steaks from the body of the shark, taking care not to lose too much blood. If the blood seeps away, the flesh stinks of ammonia. Sprinkle the steaks with salt and pepper and place them carefully into hot lard in a wide pan. Cook until the meat curls up at the edges. Serve with sauerkraut and slices of onion.

SEPTEMBER 12TH, 1768   MADEIRA

We've loaded 4,400 pounds of beef, onions (20 pounds per man), oranges, lemons and over 7,000 gallons of wine into the hold. That should do us for a while.

That said, the pests have a nose for anything in barrels or casks: we have weevils, maggots, cockroaches and rats. And the biscuits get so hard we soak them in soup or beer. (Not water, or the men'll spend all night on "the seat of ease.")

OCTOBER 25TH, 1768   THE EQUATOR

Today everyone who's never crossed the equator— dogs and cats included—was tied to a chair and dipped three times into the sea. The captain, Mr. Banks and some of the gentlemen paid with brandy to get out of the dunking.

All the men are drunk tonight, celebrating the crossing.

November 12th, 1768 RIO DE JANEIRO, BRAZIL

Seemingly, the viceroy in Rio de Janeiro thought we were all spies. Only the captain was allowed ashore. Mr. Banks was hopping mad as he wanted to go collecting. So he and Dr. Solander climbed out the cabin window and rowed ashore. They took Richmond, one of Banks's servants, because he was a trained plant collector.

A few days later, when we sailed south, Mr. Banks had a big smile on his face. He had added a beautiful hummingbird nest to his collection and made 245 entries in his pocketbook.

JANUARY 11TH, 1769   TIERRA DEL FUEGO, PATAGONIA

It's getting colder as we travel south.

Mr. Charles Clerke, master's mate, says there could well
be giants in Patagonia. He convinced the Royal Society of it.
The others are keeping their eyes peeled. My heavy wooden
spoon will do me.

JANUARY 16TH, 1769   AN UNFORTUNATE EVENT

Yesterday, Mr. Banks, Naturalist Solander, Astronomer
Green, Surgeon Monkhouse, Artist Buchan, four of
Mr. Banks's servants, and two seamen went off to
explore the interior of the island. The outing
was a disaster. Buchan had an epileptic fit.
He recovered but shortly afterwards it
began to snow. In the search for
cover, some of the party became
too exhausted to carry on and were left behind.
The others eventually spent the night in a
makeshift shelter with only the raw meat of one
vulture for their dinner. When returning to the
ship this morning, the collectors found
Richmond and Dorlton,
two of the servants,
frozen to death
in the snow.

ALBATROSS

Pull off the skin and feathers.
Soak the bird overnight in salt
water then parboil it. Throw the
water away and cut the meat up.
Stew it until tender.
Serve with prune sauce, ground
ginger and a sprinkle of sugar.
Garnish with boiled wild celery
and a sailor's biscuit.

Mr. Banks is generally well pleased with
my cooking but felt poorly after dinner.
Everyone else ate the leftovers for supper
tonight and reported them delicious.

JANUARY 25TH, 1769   PACIFIC OCEAN

We've sailed around Cape Horn and are heading
across the Pacific Ocean in a nor'westerly
direction. But the crew is not in good health.
Even Mr. Banks has ulcers in his mouth.

The onions from Madeira are all gone. Pumpkins
are finished. The only vegetable left is that stinky
German cabbage. Barrels of it! Smells worse
than the young officers' cabins. The captain has
ordered that sauerkraut be served to the whole
ship. But the crew won't touch the stuff.

FROM NOW ON SAUERKRAUT WILL BE SERVED TO OFFICERS AND GENTLEMEN ONLY!

This morning, following orders from the top, I drained the stinking cabbage into a china bowl for the big cabin. Suddenly, several other bowls appeared. The mess cooks had decided the crew deserved this officers-only sauerkraut as well. At dinner everyone from the captain to the youngest cabin boy eagerly ate their servings of German cabbage.

April 13th, 1769   MATAVAI BAY, TAHITI

Land at last! When anchors were dropped, a crowd of canoes surrounded us. Two of the natives brought gifts—chickens, a pig, coconuts, bananas, yams and breadfruit. More food, more work.

We bartered for extra provisions—a spike nail for a small pig and a white glass bead for ten coconuts.

The next afternoon, the captain and Mr. Banks were hosted at a feast, where the food was lifted from earth ovens and served on banana leaves—jellyfish, shellfish and lobsters, followed by the meat of hogs, dogs and chickens.

June 3rd, 1769 THE TRANSIT OF VENUS ACROSS THE SUN

We have been here for six weeks while the experimental gentlemen set up an observatory in Matavai Bay, called Fort Venus. It can house 45 men in tents. I believe the telescope and quadrant are the best the captain and Mr. Green could buy.

Today the purpose of our journey arrived: the chance to watch the planet Venus cross the Sun. Unfortunately the view of the planet wasn't as clear as they had hoped. Well, worse things have happened at sea and I have more important things on my plate. Pease porridge hot with breadfruit...

This morning, the captain told me to get the fire good and hot. He had seen a very fat goose and an even fatter turkey that set his mouth watering. But he couldn't persuade the Tahitians to let him take them for his table. HMS *Dolphin* left the fowl behind some years ago, and they've become pets.

It has been hard on the locals, feeding over 80 extra mouths for three months. Our men have gathered fruit and vegetables as well as fish, birds, turtles and shellfish. We didn't realise we were stealing from the Tahitians.

While we were stealing from the Tahitians, they were stealing from us. The ship is constantly raided for tools and nails, even the glass from the portholes. The captain's quadrant went missing and, today, so did the iron rake I use in the oven.

The Tahitians have men's fruit trees and women's fruit trees. Food for men of high standing is cooked separately and senior men eat alone. Women and men never eat together.

July 13th, 1769

We sailed westwards to Raiatea. The captain is anxious to get on with continent-hunting in the south, following his secret instructions from the Admiralty.

Mr. Banks has invited Tupaia, a local chief, to join the *Endeavour* for the remainder of the voyage. He is renowned as a navigator but doesn't believe there is a great continent to be discovered. He came on board today with his servant, Taiata.

TUPAIA

TAIATA

THE LETTER FROM THE ADMIRALTY

October 6th, 1769 NEW ZEALAND

Half past one in the afternoon—I looked up from cleaning the bell—LAND!

I was about to shout "Land ahoy!" when the surgeon's boy, Nicholas Young, beat me to it.

In the afternoon, the *Endeavour* sailed into what the captain has called Poverty Bay. "A poor name for a poor place," he said. I suppose he thought there was no food for us there.

We continued south but couldn't find a good anchorage. So we turned back north at a point the captain has named Cape Turnagain.

Christmas Eve 1769

At sunset we spotted Three Kings Islands. Abel Tasman, the Dutchman, named them when he saw the islands lined up like the three wise men on the 12th night of Christmas away back in 1642.

The storms had eased so I lit the fire once more. Mr. Banks took his little boat and his gun out on the calm sea. He brought back sixty gannets. You-know-who has to prepare them.

If we eat this lot we'll turn into gannets.

Yuletide Goose Pie for all the men. No pease porridge today! And double rations of rum. Hurrah!

GOOSE PIE

Cook the goose meat (gannets) in a soup of beer, rum and wine.
Let it cool and strain off the liquid.
Into the shredded meat, bind fried onions, 6 small chopped potatoes and a hefty handful of grated cheddar from Mr. Banks's private store.
Mix well and place in a deep dish.
Over the top lay a crust of pastry and bake until brown.

A few days later, I was serving dinner when we sailed past a cluster of small islands on the starboard side. The captain named them after his choicest pudding—my recipe!

Tremendous storms hit the ship as we rounded the north cape. For several days, I had to serve the men cold food. It was too dangerous to light the fires.

POOR KNIGHTS PUDDING

Beat 2 eggs with a small spoonful of sugar, cinnamon and ½ cup of milk. Pour the mixture over 4 thick slices of bread and leave to soak. Heat dripping in a pan, drain the bread and carefully slide the slices into the hot fat. Fry until golden brown.

JANUARY 1ST, 1770

Sailing down the west coast, we pass the noblest hill I've ever seen— a brown sugar mountain drizzled with icing. And I am the first to spy it. This is my chance.

We are snug at anchor in an inlet the gentlemen have named Ship Cove. It's an ideal place to gather vegetables, fish and fresh water and to repair our ship.

I have been observing the local food. The Maori roast small birds, fish and rats over a fire. They cook large fish and dogs in pit ovens, on heated rocks covered with earth. They heat fern root over a fire then beat it on a stone with a wooden hammer until the skin comes off. The Maori will have none of our rum and drink only water.

PEASE PORRIDGE
AND CELERY GRASS

To a pot of pease porridge made in the ordinary way, add 50 handfuls of chopped celery grass. Let it stand until the greens are thoroughly wilted.

Kiore

The captain tells us he traded a bag of sugar with a Maori woman for all her family treasures. She carried the sugar to the top of the hill and poured it in a creek to make the water sweet. She called it Waireka (Sweet Water). A cook could have told her what her sugar was worth—but the officers don't hesitate to take what they want.

Visiting our ship yesterday, some Maori thought the mutton from one of our sheep was human meat, or "long pork."

Then this morning, the captain and Mr. Banks found a human arm and other human bones in a food basket on a nearby beach. The Maori said they belonged to enemies. Our men were horrified and named the place Cannibal Cove. Old seafaring tales of people-eaters at the edge of the world are evidently true.

Planks and ropes have been put out from the *Endeavour* to encourage our rats to make their home on the mainland.

FEBRUARY 1770

With repairs complete, and a good supply of wild celery and dried fish, we left Ship Cove and sailed north-east through a wide strait.

"Thompson's Strait" perhaps...

Now it was time to turn south along the east coast of the island the Maori call Te Wai Pounamu. Well—I hardly care what they call it.

TE WAI POUNAMU

SOUTH ISLAND!

MARCH 10TH, 1770

The *Endeavour* rounded a small island at the southern end of the country. Many of the officers and gentlemen are disappointed to learn that New Zealand is simply three large islands. We have not found the Great Southern Continent.

RAKIURA

For Mr. Banks and several other continent-mongers, such was their disappointment that they were sick after supper. Can't blame my leftover dog pie!

COOK'S STRAIT!

We returned to Cape Turnagain. We had sailed right round an island.

TE IKA A MAUI

NORTH ISLAND!

How about "Thompson's Island"...?

Near the southern end of New Zealand, to celebrate Lieutenant John Gore's birthday, I was told to come up with something special for the gentlemen's supper.

"Salted pork, pease porridge, or both?" I asked.

"Dog!" said Mr. Green. "A feast of dog!"

So a feast they were given. Roasted hindquarters, forequarters in a pie and the guts made into haggis.

Stocks of sugar, salt, tea and tobacco are very low, with only enough for 6 months on 2/3 rations. I reckon it's time to head home.

AOTEAROA

The captain seemed to think the same as me. Perhaps he was also tired of dragging the salted meat behind the ship to soften it up. We sailed up the west coast of New Zealand past Cape Foulwind to Admiralty Bay, where we restocked with water, wood, local vegetables and fish. On March 31st we continued past Cape Farewell and westwards towards Van Diemen's Land.

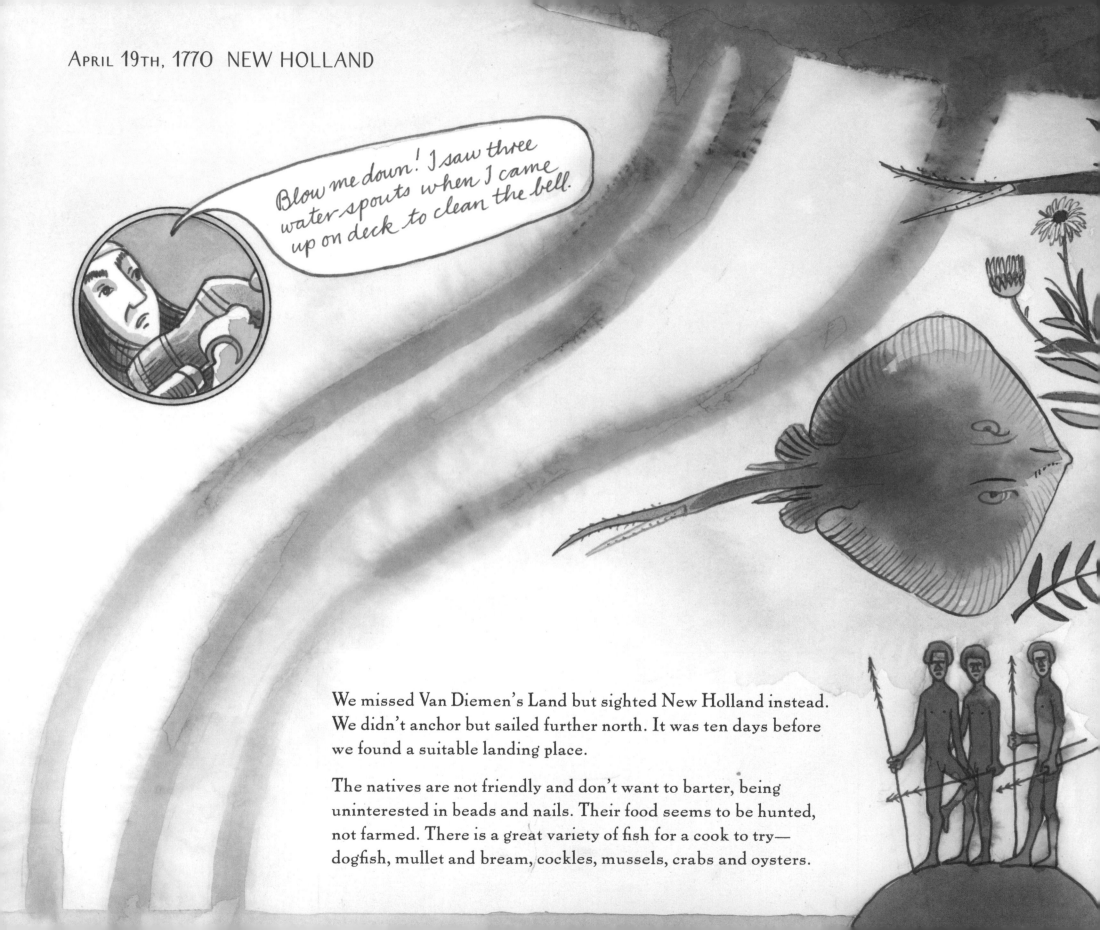

We missed Van Diemen's Land but sighted New Holland instead. We didn't anchor but sailed further north. It was ten days before we found a suitable landing place.

The natives are not friendly and don't want to barter, being uninterested in beads and nails. Their food seems to be hunted, not farmed. There is a great variety of fish for a cook to try— dogfish, mullet and bream, cockles, mussels, crabs and oysters.

The officers have called the bay Stingray Harbour after the huge number caught in the yawl on our last day there. Of course I came up with a recipe.

STINGRAY SOUP

Skin, bone and cube the stingray.
Cover it with water in a wide pan. Add salt and bring to the boil. Simmer for an hour.
Add two large ladles of sauerkraut and simmer for another hour.
Serve over crushed biscuits.

NOT STINGRAY HARBOUR—
BOTANY BAY!

Mr. Banks and Mr. Solander collected so many plants that they had to spread a sail on the beach to lay out their specimens to dry.

As the ship sailed northwards, the coast became more dangerous with small islands and hidden reefs cropping up regularly.

Late one night, as I was draining the meat for the next day's dinner, we struck a reef. Everyone took to the pumps, including Mr. Banks.

Next morning we threw 50 tons of cannons, ballast, casks, oil jars and decayed stores overboard so the *Endeavour* could be refloated. The hole in the hull was sealed with a fother.

A few days later, the ship quietly sailed into what we named Weary Bay.

I am cooking on shore over open fires. Done the right way, kangaroo is good to eat.

The ship's carpenters will need several weeks here for repairs. Mr. Banks fills his time shooting wildlife.

Catching turtles has become a new sport. Cooking them is another. Twelve have been brought back to the ship, the flesh divided equally by weight amongst the entire crew.

KANGAROO STEW

Roughly chop half a dozen kangaroo tails, onions,
a pound of potatoes and a handful of wild sage.
Place all in a heavy pot with a dash of salt
and a spoonful of peppercorns.
Cook until the meat is soft.
Thicken the gravy with flour.
Serve with biscuits or pease porridge.

TURTLE SOUP

Chop up the meat of a large turtle and add to a large pot
of water with an onion, 2 sticks of celery and stock.
Bring to the boil and simmer for 1 hour.
Once the meat is soft, add a handful of bay leaves,
2 spoonfuls of mace, the juice of a lemon and a cup
of wine. Simmer the meat for another hour.
Before serving, add the chopped, hard-boiled whites
of 2 eggs and a cup of parsley.

AUGUST 16TH, 1770

After a few false starts, the *Endeavour* has managed
to sail clear of the reef into open seas. Northwards!

OCTOBER 11TH, 1770   BATAVIA, JAVA

I've heard bad things about this place, Batavia, with its disease-carrying mosquitoes.

We have called in here so the captain can dispatch a report of his findings to the Admiralty in England. And the ship badly needs further repairs, thanks to shipworm.

But I feel it in my bones…this port of call could be our undoing.

NOVEMBER 15TH, 1770

The crew has been struck down with malaria. All but ten of us are affected. I now use a very small pot for the pease porridge.

Many have died: William Monkhouse, the surgeon, and John Reynolds, one of Banks's men. And so have Tupaia and Taiata—these Pacific navigators won't see England after all.

JANUARY 6TH, 1771

We have reached the Indian Ocean and stopped for provisions at Princes Island. But the water here is bad, so now dysentery rivals the malaria for laying us waste.

JANUARY 27TH, 1771

Sydney Parkinson, the artist, has died.

JANUARY 29TH, 1771

We have lost Charles Green, the astronomer.

More men have fallen ill, and I have joined them. I can no longer do my duties. Days are wretched and nights on the seat of ease are worse. My bowels twist and heave. I fear I can no longer hold on to this life.

JANUARY 31ST, 1771

Finally I let go.

As my corpse was slid into the sea, my soul soared up and, with a mournful cry, slipped into the body of a seagull.

MARCH 13TH, 1771
CAPE TOWN, SOUTH AFRICA

We who have departed follow the ship to see the men home, watching their progress from the rigging.

The captain purchased a whole ox as a treat for his crew, a great delicacy after our diet of the past two years.

MAY 15TH, 1771
ECLIPSE OF THE SUN

Banks's greyhound died.

With no artists left on board, the
captain and some of the officers
and gentlemen have had to make
sketches of the land we pass.
And the ship's bell is as black as
your hat now I'm not cleaning it.

It's true that the observation of the Transit
of Venus was not entirely successful and we
did not find the Great Southern Continent.

But the voyage of the *Endeavour* was one to be
proud of. Lieutenant James Cook beat scurvy
and charted New Zealand and the eastern coast
of New Holland. Thousands of plant, bird and
animal species were identified. Of our 94 crew,
56 returned to England.

Mr. Banks and Mr. Solander were the only
experimental gentlemen to survive.

Although hundreds of landmarks and waterways were given new names, mine was not attached to a single mountain or even a small hill.

But as Cook's cook, I did my job well. I made crocodile steaks, emu pie, seaweed salad and roasted rat—and, Mr. Banks told me, some of the best cuttlefish soup he ever tasted.

On that three-year voyage, I cooked up more salted pork and pease porridge than any man ever did in a lifetime—and with only one hand, what's more.

Pease porridge hot, pease porridge cold
Pease porridge in the pot nine days old
Some like it hot, some like it cold
Some like it in the pot nine days old.

THOMPSON'S PORRIDGE!

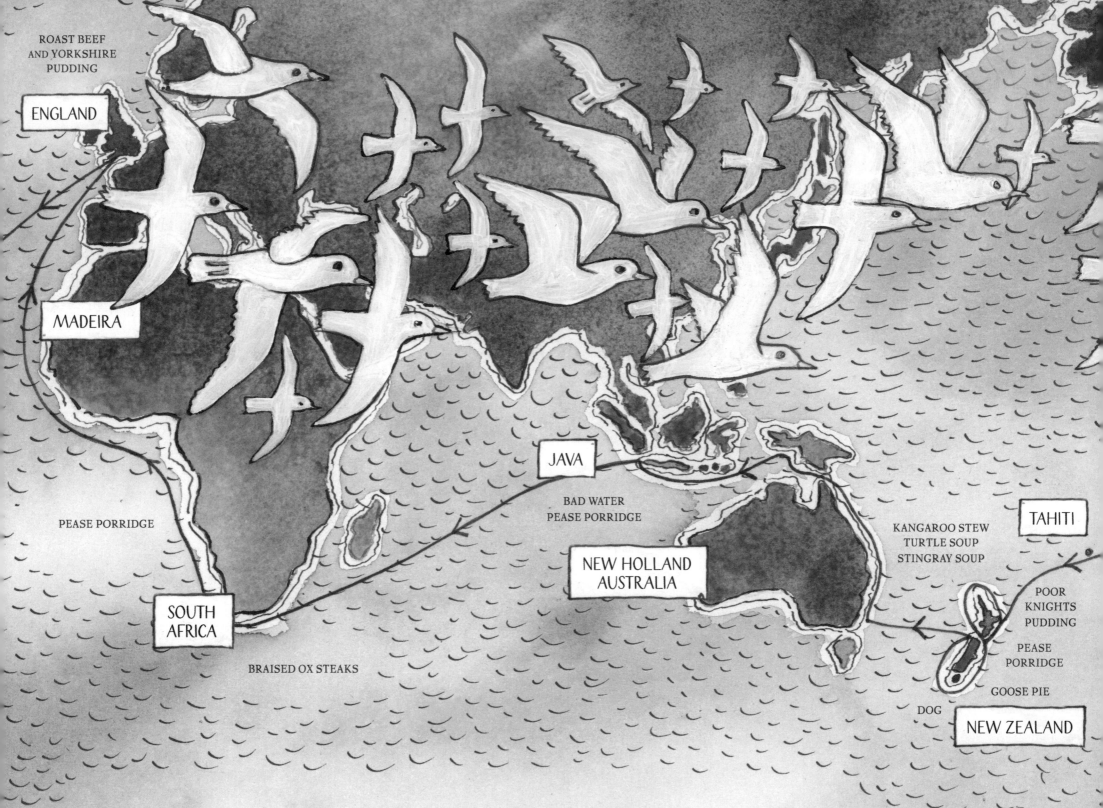

ROAST BEEF
AND YORKSHIRE
PUDDING

ENGLAND

MADEIRA

JAVA

BAD WATER
PEASE PORRIDGE

TAHITI

PEASE PORRIDGE

KANGAROO STEW
TURTLE SOUP
STINGRAY SOUP

NEW HOLLAND
AUSTRALIA

SOUTH
AFRICA

POOR
KNIGHTS
PUDDING

PEASE
PORRIDGE

BRAISED OX STEAKS

GOOSE PIE

DOG

NEW ZEALAND

COOK'S FIRST PACIFIC VOYAGE 1768–1771